TRACKING DOWN

THE VIKINGS

IN BRITAIN

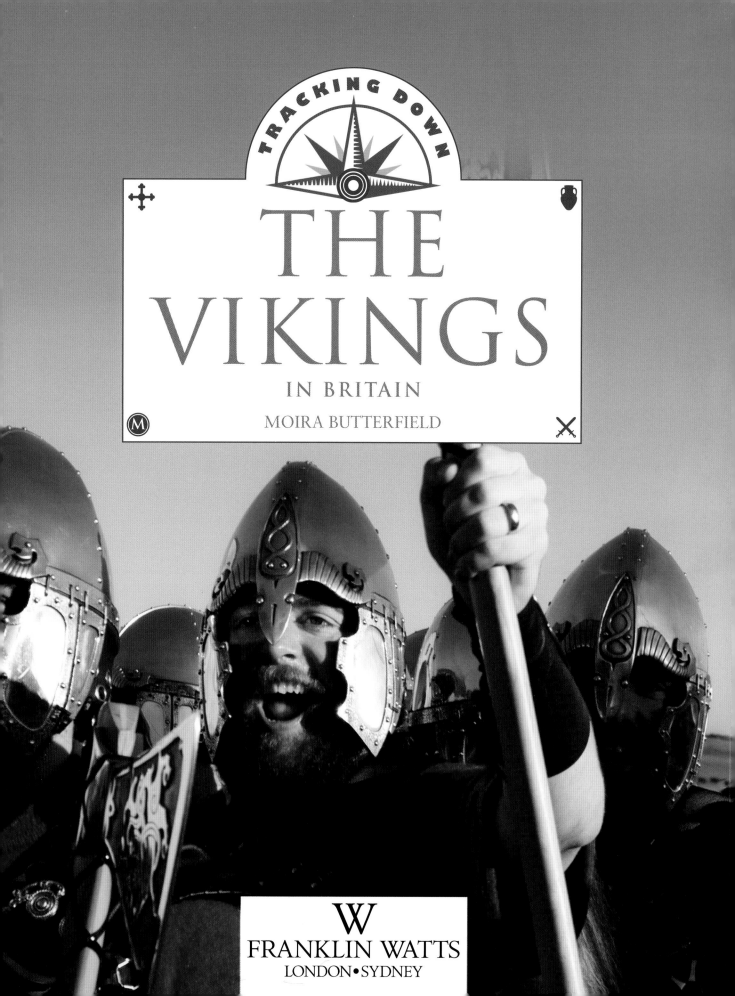

TRACKING DOWN

THE VIKINGS

IN BRITAIN

MOIRA BUTTERFIELD

W

FRANKLIN WATTS

LONDON • SYDNEY

First published in 2010 by Franklin Watts

Copyright © 2010 Franklin Watts

Franklin Watts
338 Euston Road
London NW1 3BH

Franklin Watts Australia
Level 17/207 Kent Street
Sydney, NSW 2000

A CIP catalogue record for this book is available
from the British Library.

Dewey number: 941'.01

ISBN 978 0 7496 9234 6

Printed in China

Franklin Watts is a division of Hachette Children's Books,
an Hachette UK company.

www.hachette.co.uk

Editor: Sarah Ridley
Design: John Christopher/White Design
Editor in Chief: John C. Miles
Art director: Jonathan Hair
Picture research: Diana Morris

Picture credits: British Library, London/Art Archive: 11b. The Trustees of the British Museum London: 20.
British Museum London/Susan James: 21. Derby Museum & Art Gallery: 12, 13t. Werner Forman
Archive: 7bl, 9b, 10, 29t, 30. Les Gibson/Alamy: 14. Rolf Hicker/Alamy: 9t. DougHoughton.com: 28.
Doug Houghton/Alamy: front cover, 8. Interfoto/Alamy: 24. Manx National Heritage: 19tc, 19tr, 22, 23t,
23c, 25c, 25r. David Muenker/Alamy: 15t. Museum of London: 26, 27t, 27c, 27b. Orkneypics/Alamy:
29b. Picturepoint/Topham: 11t. David Robertson/Alamy: 7tr. John Robertson/Alamy: 6.
Shetland Museum Archives: 15b. Doug Steley/Alamy: 18. Tim Walton/Awe Inspiring Images/PD: 19bl.
York Archaeological Trust: 16, 17t, 17b. *Every attempt has been made to clear copyright.*
Should there be any inadvertent omission please apply to the publisher for rectification.

CONTENTS

VIKINGS IN BRITAIN

In the 8th century, bloodthirsty raiders began sailing to Britain from Norway, Sweden and Denmark. They were given the name 'Vikings', which means 'sea pirates'. At first they attacked, stole whatever they could find, and went home. But eventually a whole army arrived and conquered parts of the country.

Attack!

The first terrifying Viking raids began in 793CE (see pages 10-11). The people living in England at this time were called Anglo-Saxons. They were Christian, but the early Viking raiders were not. They attacked Christian monasteries, which were undefended and had valuable treasures inside. They killed monks, stole treasure and set fire to the buildings. They also attacked villages, killing the locals or taking them home as slaves.

➜ Dressed for battle, this man is wearing a replica Viking helmet and carrying a replica sword. These are copies of real Viking artefacts discovered by archaeologists.

Vikings come to stay

In 865CE a massive Viking army arrived from Denmark and conquered northern, central and eastern England. But in 878CE the Anglo-Saxon king, Alfred of Wessex, managed to stop the advance by defeating the Vikings in battle. He made an agreement to draw a boundary between his land and their kingdom, which was named the Danelaw. Meanwhile, Norwegian Vikings settled in northern and western Scotland, parts of Wales and the Isle of Man in the Irish Sea.

↑ A scene in the Shetland Islands, north of Scotland, one of the areas settled by Vikings. The houses have thick walls and small windows to keep the heat in during winter.

GO VISIT

⚔ Viking settlements

In the Danelaw, the area the Vikings once ruled, you can often tell you're visiting an old Viking settlement by its name. Typical Viking placenames end with -by, -thorpe, -toft, -thwaite, -holme and -kirk. Look on a map of north and east England to spot them.

➔ Historians study the many Viking objects found in Britain, such as this coin, to build up a picture of Viking life.

Fighting again

The Vikings who had come to Britain became Christian and in England their land was gradually reconquered by Alfred's son and grandson. But in the 10th century, Danish Vikings began to attack England again (see page 26). For a while they were paid off with ransom money, but eventually they conquered the whole of England. The Danish King Cnut became King of England, and his relatives ruled until 1066.

PEOPLE IN VIKING BRITAIN

The first Viking raiders were warriors, looking for treasure and slaves. But once they had conquered land, many Vikings settled down with their families and became farmers, or lived and worked in towns.

➜ A re-enactor wears an authentic replica Viking helmet. Only the wealthiest warriors would have worn metal helmets as they took a great deal of skill to make.

Fearsome fighters

Viking warriors were fearsome fighters armed with iron spears, swords or battle-axes, and a wooden shield. They wore a helmet with ear flaps and a long nose piece hanging down the front. Modern pictures of Vikings often show them wearing helmets with horns on top, but there is no evidence that this was true. We do know that Vikings admired great warriors, and their ancient tales often feature fighting heroes.

↑ These historical re-enactors show the kind of clothes Vikings wore in summer.

What Vikings looked like

Viking men wore tunics, trousers and a belt. Women wore a headscarf and a long dress with a pinafore over the top. Both men and women wore leather shoes and had cloaks to keep them warm. Their clothes were made from woollen cloth spun by hand and coloured with dyes made from plants. Vikings liked wearing jewellery such as silver arm rings and brooch pins.

Viking workers

Many Viking settlers became farmers or craftsmen. The farmers grew their own crops and kept their own animals. Their whole family would have lived together in one or two rooms in a long narrow farmhouse, which they probably shared with their animals (see pages 14-15). Viking children did not go to school. They would have worked alongside their parents as soon as they were old enough.

GO VISIT

Viking treasures

Here are some typical Viking finds. Look out for them in local and national museums.

Coins
Viking-age coins marked with dates help historians to work out when Vikings visited a place.

Stones and crosses
Viking-style decorations carved on stones are a sign that Vikings once lived in an area.

Buried treasure
Archaeologists have found buried jewellery (such as the pendant, right), weapons and hoards of treasure (see pages 20-21).

TERROR FROM THE SEA

In 793 monks living on the island of Lindisfarne, Northumberland, were massacred in one of the very first Viking raids on Britain. Screaming warriors charged up from the shore towards Lindisfarne Priory, intent on murder and destruction.

A murderous surprise

The raid on Lindisfarne Priory was a terrible shock to the rest of the country, especially because it was thought to be a very holy site. The Vikings were after church treasure such as silver candlesticks and the jewels which were often fixed onto the covers of Bibles at that time. According to later descriptions of the raid, they murdered some Lindisfarne monks and took others as slaves.

↓The ruins of Lindisfarne Priory today. Some of these date from long after the time of the Viking raid in 793.

Scary ships

The Viking warriors arrived in longships, long narrow warships powered by oars or a single square sail. The longships were tough and flexible so they could survive in heavy seas, but they were also shallow enough to sail up rivers. The prow of a longship was curled upwards and carved into a fearsome dragon. Parts of the ship were painted gold, which glittered from afar.

Lindisfarne and the *Lindisfarne Gospels*

You can visit the ruined priory on Lindisfarne, also called Holy Island, or see its most famous treasure, the *Lindisfarne Gospels*, at the British Library in London (or on its website, see page 31). This beautifully hand-painted book probably began life with a jewel-encrusted cover but that has disappeared. Perhaps the Vikings stole it, leaving the book itself behind. The gospels are part of the Bible.

⬆ The Lindisfarne Priory Stone, part of a grave marker. It is carved with Viking warriors in search of plunder and brandishing weapons.

Writers tell all

Anglo-Saxon writers later told the tale of what happened at Lindisfarne. They said that the Vikings came to Britain: "like stinging hornets… like ravening wolves, plundering, devouring, slaughtering," [and [from then on], "there was warfare and sorrow in England." These accounts were written by monks hundreds of years after the raid, but the thought of it still seemed to shock and scare them.

⬅ A beautifully hand-decorated page from the *Lindisfarne Gospels*.

11

A GREAT ARMY

In 865 a big Viking army arrived from Denmark and landed in eastern England. They wanted to conquer land and settle it for themselves. For 14 years they rampaged across the country, fighting in summer and camping in winter. One of their winter camps was at Repton in Derbyshire.

Winter waiting

We know from Anglo-Saxon records that the Great Army stayed at Repton in the winter of 873. They piled up earth to make a defensive bank around a site by a river, and used an old Anglo-Saxon church as their headquarters. They buried their dead in and around the church buildings, but in a pagan style. Many of the Viking bodies found there seem to have died from natural causes, so perhaps the camp was an unhealthy disease-ridden place.

← Forensic archaeologists used measurements taken from the skull of a Viking warrior killed at Repton to reconstruct his face in clay. They will have guessed at the beard and eye colour.

The grave of a Viking warrior found at Repton

Archaeologists found several Viking graves at the east end of the church. One of these was a warrior who had been killed in battle.

This man was killed by a massive cut at the top of his left thigh. He was aged about 35-40, and was 1.82m (6ft) tall.

He was buried with weapons and equipment including a sword and a small silver hammer, the symbol of the Viking god Thor.

A young man aged about 17-20 was buried alongside the warrior. The young man had an iron knife. The double grave was marked with a timber post and covered by a setting of stones.

A gold ring from a Viking woman's grave

The tusk of a wild boar was placed between the man's thighs. The thigh bone of a jackdaw was found in an area of softer earth, which may once have been a box or bag placed between the man's legs.

Thor's rods were worn as lucky charms

This bronze belt buckle was found at the man's waist. It has traces of textile and leather.

The iron sword lay beside the man's left leg. It is sheathed in a wooden scabbard which was lined with fleece and covered in leather. The scabbard was...

Death by sword

In the churchyard archaeologists found the graves of two warriors who had been killed by sword blows. They were buried with clothing, weapons and lucky charms. Vikings believed that warriors who died in battle would go to a heavenly feasting hall called Valhalla, and would need their clothes and weapons in the afterlife.

Follow the leaders

The Great Army did not have one main leader. Instead there were several different kings and earls, called 'jarls'. Bands of Vikings were loyal to their own particular leader, and would fight to the death for him.

⬆ A sword found in a Viking grave at Repton.

GO VISIT

Derby Museum and Art Gallery

At Derby Museum and Art Gallery you can see the treasures found at Repton, among the Viking burials. These include swords and battle-axes, a skull that was smashed in battle, silver coins dating to the time of the Great Army, and a silver lucky charm in the shape of Thor's hammer. Thor was the Viking god of thunder.

A VIKING FARM

The remains of Viking farm buildings have been uncovered at Jarlshof on the southern tip of Shetland in Scotland. Norwegian Vikings farmed there, on the site of an older Pictish settlement. No-one knows what happened to the Picts who lived there before the Viking ships appeared.

Longhouse with sauna

The Vikings built houses that were long and narrow, called longhouses. They had stone walls and wooden roofs with turf laid on top. There were seven Viking houses at Jarlshof. The oldest one measured 20m by 7m and had two rooms inside. Outside there was a byre for animals, a smithy and a building that might have been an early sauna, where water was thrown on to warm stones to make steam.

▼ Some of the remains of the Viking settlement at Jarlshof in Shetland.

Longhouse life

There were benches along each long side of the house, for sitting or sleeping on. In the middle there was a fire for heating and cooking. It must have been smoky and dark in the house. Smelly candles made of animal fat would have glowed in the gloom. The family would have passed the time indoors spinning wool, making tools and listening to sagas — tales of Norwegian heroes. At night they probably wrapped themselves in animal furs to keep warm.

↑ A reconstruction of the inside of a Viking longhouse.

GO VISIT

Jarlshof settlement and Shetland Museum

You can visit the Jarlshof site on Shetland, and see some of its treasures at the Shetland Museum in Lerwick. These include a slate tablet scratched with a picture of a longship and slate tablets scratched with pictures of people – a young man with a beard and curly hair, and an older man in a high-collared tunic.

→ Part of a Viking comb found at Jarlshof. It is made from animal bone.

Farming folk

The Viking farmers at Jarlshof grew wheat and rye to make bread, barley to make beer and oats for porridge. They kept sheep, cattle and pigs, and also ate fish and seal meat. They probably grew vegetables such as cabbage and onions and made their own butter and cheese. We know what kind of animals they ate because they threw the animal bones away in a rubbish heap and modern archaeologists have found them.

A VIKING TOWN

The Vikings took over the towns they conquered. They made Jorvik, now called York, the capital of their territory. It became the second biggest city in the country, after London, and was ruled by Viking kings until 954.

Busy builders

The Vikings repaired the walls that the Romans had built around the town, and they added new streets and houses. There were soon lots of craft workshops and a busy waterfront where goods were sent or bought from around the Viking world. Jorvik was an important centre for buying and selling, though the Vikings did not use money until around 1000. Instead they paid for things with scraps of silver (see page 20) or they bartered (swapped) one thing for another.

▼ Pieces from a Viking board game found in York, called 'Hnefatafl', which means 'King's table'.

All sorts of skills

We know what some of the craftsmen of Jorvik made because archaeologists have found lots of their tools and materials. There were blacksmiths who made all kinds of metal objects, such as swords. Jewellers created beautiful brooches and rings using fine silver and gold wire. There were glass-blowers, leather workers, woodcarvers and craftsmen who carved objects from deer antlers and animal bone.

▲ A soft leather Viking shoe found in York, fitted onto a piece of animal bone to make an ice-skate.

GO VISIT

Jorvik Viking Centre, York

At the Jorvik Viking Centre you can find out how Vikings lived in the city and see treasures, such as this amber jewellery. The amber came from faraway Baltic lands.

Damp doings

In the area of York called Coppergate the earth is spongy and damp, and these conditions have preserved the remains of Viking houses and thousands of everyday Viking objects from the 900s. From these we know how the local Vikings lived, and even what made them itch. Lots of flea and human lice remains have been found littering the floors. The damp conditions preserved leather shoes and pieces of clothing. Archaeologists even found Viking human faeces from toilet pits, along with the moss and wool fragments they used instead of toilet paper.

VIKING LAWS

In Viking-controlled parts of Britain people had to abide by Viking law. Vikings had regular gatherings called 'Things' or 'Althings', when laws were explained and every free Viking adult had the right to speak.

↓ Dressed in replica Viking finery, this couple are re-enacting a Viking wedding.

Marriage meetings

When an Althing was held Vikings came from miles around. It was a chance for families to meet up and hear the latest news, and it was also a chance to find someone to marry. For Viking families living in the far north, it would have been an especially rare chance to meet new people.

The Tynwald

The Norwegian Vikings who settled on the Isle of Man held a 'Tynwald', a summer meeting when laws were read out and agreed to. The Tynwald still meets to pass laws on the Isle of Man, and is one of the oldest parliaments in the world. In addition to its usual meetings, it meets on the hilltop site of the old Tynwald on 5th July. The island was Norwegian until 1266, long after Viking rule ended in England.

→ Tynwald Hill, the original site of the Viking Tynwald. On 5th July, an open-air sitting of the Manx (Isle of Man) parliament takes place on the hilltop.

At the Manx Museum in Douglas you can see some of the Viking treasures found on the Isle of Man, where the Tynwald is still held. These include fragments of a rare bronze Viking sword dating from 900, a hoard of silver treasure including a broken silver armlet, and a beautiful bead necklace that belonged to an important Viking woman, nicknamed the 'Pagan Lady of Peel', who was buried at Peel Castle on the Isle of Man.

▲ The finely decorated fragments of the sword in the Manx Museum.

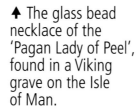

▲ The glass bead necklace of the 'Pagan Lady of Peel', found in a Viking grave on the Isle of Man.

Feuds and punishment

At an Althing, disputes between Vikings were judged and punishments decided. The parliament might have had to judge the case of a thief or a murderer, for example. Vikings were known for having violent long-running family feuds that often led to murders. Punishments for Viking crimes were harsh and included drowning or having a hand cut off.

VIKING TREASURE

In 1840 workmen digging in Cuerdale, Lancashire, discovered one of the biggest hoards of Viking silver treasure ever found. You can see part of the Cuerdale Hoard at the British Museum in London. Other buried treasure hoards have been discovered around the Viking world.

➤ Some of the silver items found in the Cuerdale Hoard. See if you can spot some coins and a belt buckle.

A big burial

At Cuerdale more than 8,600 silver items were buried in a lead chest. There were thousands of silver coins, along with jewellery, buckles, ingots (silver shaped into bars) and chopped-up silver pieces called 'hack-silver'. Vikings used pieces of hack-silver instead of money, weighing it to work out what it was worth.

Cuerdale Hoard at the British Museum

At the British Museum you can see coins from the hoard. They came from lots of different places, including Arabia and Russia, as well as newly-made coins from York. The owner got them either by stealing or from trading in goods.

← In amongst the coins were these cloak pins, used to fasten garments.

Who buried it?

From the dates of the coins in the hoard, it's thought the treasure was buried between 905 and 910. This was just after Vikings had been driven out of Dublin in Ireland. The treasure was buried next to a river that was a main route to Ireland from York, and a lot of the silver came from Ireland, so it's possible the defeated Irish Vikings buried it.

Why bury it?

No-one knows for sure why Vikings buried treasure. The most likely reason was to keep it safe in troubled times. Then perhaps it was forgotten or its owner died. Another theory is that the Vikings may have believed it was possible for someone who had died to use treasure in the afterlife.

SHIPPED TO HEAVEN

The first Vikings to settle in Britain were pagan. They believed in lots of different gods and goddesses instead of the Christian god in the Bible. Important pagan Vikings were buried in ships along with their possessions, which Vikings believed they took to the next life.

Boat tombs

Evidence of ship burials is rare in Britain, but a few have been discovered on the Isle of Man. The remains of one can still be seen at Balladoole, where a man was buried in a wooden boat under a mound of earth. The outline of the boat was marked in stones around the mound. The boat's wooden planking has rotted away underground but it left behind 300 nails still in position, so we can tell that it was about 11m long.

↓ The burial site at Balladoole, with the boat outline towards the bottom of the photograph.

The skull of the man from Balladoole has been used to recreate his face as a computerised image. You can come face to face with him at the Manx Museum, along with some of his treasures, including his broken sword and wooden shield fragments, once painted red, black and white.

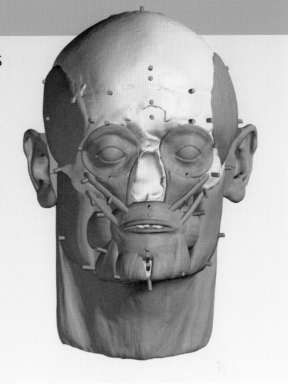

➜ A sword decorated with silver, deliberately broken into pieces before being buried at Balladoole.

⬆ The Balladoole man – the computerised image of his face, on display at the Manx Museum, Isle of Man.

Sacrifice secret

At Balladoole the man was buried with items he might need in his afterlife, such as a shield and a cauldron. And a young woman was buried nearby. It's not clear whether she was a human sacrifice, but we know that people (possibly slaves) were sometimes sacrificed and buried with high-ranking Vikings. In another nearby Viking burial at Ballateare, a woman was buried alongside a rich Viking man and, from her remains, we can tell she was killed by a swordblow to the head.

Viking heaven and hell

Pagan Vikings believed in three worlds. Earth was called Midgard. Under Earth was Nifelheim, a misty frozen wasteland. Above the Earth was Asgard, home of the gods. In Asgard there was a magnificent building, a 'great hall', called Valhalla, where only warriors who died in battle could go for a glorious afterlife of feasting and drinking. Vikings passed on their beliefs in stories and poetry, recited in their own homes or in great halls belonging to high-ranking Vikings.

ALPHABET AND ART

At Old Kirk Braddan, on the Isle of Man, there is a fine collection of ancient stones decorated with curling beasts and mysterious-looking symbols. The symbols are runes, the alphabet of the Vikings, and the carvings are Viking art.

Useful runes

Runes represent letters in the Viking alphabet. The Vikings carved them on stones and objects, but didn't write them down on paper. They were used as inscriptions on memorial stones or to label objects with the owner's name. Occasionally they were also used to carve magic curses or healing spells on pieces of bone, to call up the magical powers of the gods.

GO VISIT

Viking graffiti on Orkney

At Maeshowe, on the island of Orkney, Vikings broke into an ancient Stone Age tomb and wrote 30 graffiti messages on the walls in runes. One wrote, 'Ingigerd is the loveliest woman'. Another added, 'Haermund Hardaxe carved these runes'.

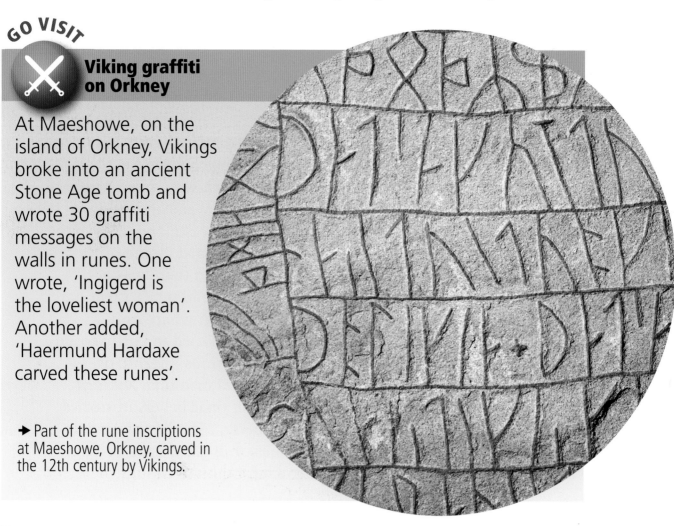

➜ Part of the rune inscriptions at Maeshowe, Orkney, carved in the 12th century by Vikings.

Beautiful beasts

The stones at Old Kirk Braddan were decorated with made-up beasts. Their long snake-like bodies weave around each other to make complicated patterns. This is typical of Viking art, used to decorate stones and objects such as swords and jewellery. The beasts were imaginary mixtures of fierce creatures such as snakes, dragons, wolves and ravens.

➔ The carved stones at Old Kirk Braddan were erected in memory of dead Vikings.

← Thorleif Knakki's Cross in Old Kirk Braddan is beautifully carved with scenes from Viking stories.

Dragons mix with crosses

Gradually Viking settlers became Christian, and their carvings help to prove it. The carvings at Old Kirk Braddan, and in other parts of Britain, show how they slowly began to alter their religion. At first they combined their old Viking art style with Christian symbols, including the cross, in the same carvings. They began marrying local Christians, too. On the Isle of Man the names on Viking tombs show that they married into local island families.

TERROR RETURNS

In England, the English kings fought back and regained Viking land in the 900s, but from 980 Danish Vikings began their raids once again. Many towns were attacked and destroyed, including London. Weapons from this violent time are on display at the Museum of London.

➤ Found in the graveyard of St Paul's Cathedral, London, this carved Viking grave marker shows a lion fighting with a snake.

Danish London

London was besieged and burnt by Danish Vikings a number of times. It was a particularly dangerous war zone because the Danes could easily sail their fleets up the Thames to the town. Finally, in 1016, it fell under the control of Viking King Cnut and was ruled by Danes for the next 25 years, when Edward the Confessor became king of both the Saxons and Danes in 1042.

Wet weapons

When London Bridge was being repaired in the 1920s workmen found Viking battle-axes and spears that had been thrown into the River Thames near the bridge. They were either dropped during fighting or perhaps thrown in as an offering to the gods after a victory. Weapons have been found in rivers all over the Viking world, but no-one knows why they were there.

Fighting Viking-style

Vikings were taught how to handle weapons from an early age. The most skilled were said to be able to throw two spears at once, and even catch a spear in flight. Warriors gave their prized swords nicknames such as 'leg-biter' and 'gold hilt'. The best-quality ones were made of steel imported from Afghanistan and Iran.

GO VISIT Museum of London

Viking treasures from the time of King Cnut are on display at the Museum of London. These include coins that show the head of King Cnut, and battle-axes from the River Thames, probably owned by warriors onboard Danish war fleets of the early 1000s. You can also see the grave slab (shown left) that commemorates someone from King Cnut's court. It is carved with runes and a picture of a lion fighting a snake.

↓ Viking iron spears and axes found in the River Thames and on display at the Museum of London.

VIKINGS GO TO CHURCH

Gradually the old Viking pagan way of life died out. Viking rulers became Christian and even built churches. In the Orkneys the Norwegian Viking earls built a round church called Orphir Round Kirk and a cathedral in Kirkwall dedicated to a Viking saint.

Old and new

Orphir Round Kirk was probably modelled on a church in Jerusalem. The Viking Earl Hakon is said to have built it in the 1100s after going on a pilgrimage to the Holy Land. Nearby are the remains of a manor house and a Great Hall, where the Orkney earls would have feasted with their warriors in the traditional Viking way.

▼ The remains of the Orphir Round Kirk in Orkney. Much of its building stone was used to build the nearby parish church in the 18th century.

Look out for Viking treasures found in churches built by the Vikings. At Brompton in Yorkshire, and other churches mainly in northern England and Scotland, you can find hogsback grave markers for Viking tombs. They are carved with wolves, bears or dogs and named because they are curved like a pig's back. They were laid horizontally over the top of the tomb like a roof.

⬆ A Viking hogsback grave marker in a church in Lancashire.

Murder and magic

Earl Hakon appears in a saga of Orkney history called the *Orkneyinga Saga*, a tale that mixes Viking history with murder, magic and adventure. It was created at the end of the 1100s by an Icelandic storyteller. In the saga Hakon is said to have had his brother Magnus killed. Magnus became a Christian saint after miracles were said to have happened at his tomb, and the cathedral at Kirkwall in Orkney is named after him.

➡ A statue of St Magnus in the cathedral at Kirkwall.

A Danish saint

In London, there are still churches named after the Viking Saint Olaf. He is the patron saint of Norway because he is credited with converting the country to Christianity. He was King of Norway between 1015 and 1028, and was a friend of King Cnut. He was more of a violent Viking warrior than a saintly man during his lifetime, though. He attacked London, and was also said to have killed or banished any Norwegians who would not convert to Christianity.

GLOSSARY

Afterlife Life after death, a belief held by many religious people.

Althing A Viking parliament, where Vikings gathered to discuss laws and disputes.

Amber An orange-yellow fossil resin used to make some Viking jewellery.

Anglo-Saxons Christian rulers of England at the time of the Viking attacks.

Armlet A bracelet worn high on the arm. Vikings liked wearing armlets.

Asgard Heavenly home of the Viking gods.

Bartering Swapping goods instead of paying for them with money. Vikings sometimes bartered.

Byre A farm building for keeping animals.

Cauldron A large metal cooking pot.

Danelaw Viking-ruled kingdom in the north, east and centre of England.

Gospels Sections of the New Testament part of the Bible. The Lindisfarne Gospels is a beautifully decorated book from Lindisfarne, a monastery raided by the Vikings.

Hack-silver Chopped-up pieces of silver used as money by Vikings.

Hoard A hidden pile of valuable items.

Hogsback A type of Viking grave marker laid over a tomb. The stone was curved like a pig's back, and carved with decorations.

Holy Land The ancient kingdom of Palestine in the Bible.

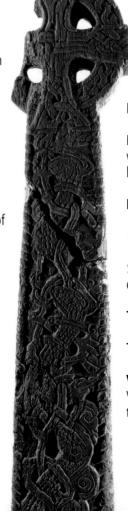

Jarl A Viking earl (nobleman).

Longhouse A long narrow Viking house with a couple of rooms inside.

Longship A long narrow Viking boat powered by oars or a sail.

Midgard The name of the Earth, according to Viking beliefs.

Monastery A religious building where Christian monks live and worship. Early Vikings attacked monasteries to steal treasure.

Nifelheim A misty frozen underworld according to Viking beliefs.

Norse The language of the Norwegian Vikings who settled in Scotland and the Isle of Man.

Odin Viking god of war.

Pagan religion A pre-Christian religion based on the worship of nature and ancestors.

Picts Tribes who lived in eastern and northern Scotland before the Vikings arrived.

Priory A type of monastery.

Prow The front of a ship. On Viking longships the prow was curved upwards and carved with a fearsome dragon head.

Runes Viking symbols that represent letters.

Saga Viking tale of heroes and gods.

Ship burial A burial in a wooden boat under a mound of earth.

Thor Viking god of thunder.

Tynwald Parliament on the Isle of Man.

Valhalla A great hall in the Viking heaven of Asgard. Vikings believed that warriors who died in battle went to Valhalla to feast and drink for ever.

PLACES TO VISIT

British Museum
Great Russell Street
London WC1B 3DG
www.britishmuseum.org

Derby Museum and Art Gallery
The Strand
Derby DE1 1BS
*www.derby.gov.uk/LeisureCulture/MuseumsGalleries/
Derby_Museum_and_Art_Gallery.htm*

Jarlshof Viking farmsteads
Sumburgh
Shetland ZE3 9JN
Scotland
www.historic-scotland.gov.uk/

Jorvik Viking Centre
Coppergate ,
York Y01 9WT
www.jorvik-viking-centre.co.uk

St Magnus Cathedral
Kirkwall
Orkney
Scotland

Lindisfarne Heritage Centre
Marygate
Holy Island
Berwick-upon-Tweed TD15 2SD
www.lindisfarne.org.uk/hicdt/museum.htm

Lindisfarne Priory
Holy Island
Northumberland
TD15 2RX
www.english-heritage.org.uk/server/show/nav.13257

Manx Museum
Kingswood Grove
Douglas
IM1 3LY
Isle of Man
*www.gov.im/mnh/heritage/museums/
manxmuseum.xml*

Museum of London
150 London Wall
London
EC2Y 5HN
www.museumoflondon.org.uk

Old Kirk Braddan
Near Douglas
Isle of Man

Tormiston Mill Visitor Centre
(for Maeshowe and Viking runes)
Orkney
KW16 3HA
www.historic-scotland.gov.uk

WEBLINKS
Here are some websites with information about Vikings in Britain.
www.bbc.co.uk/history/ancient/vikings/
All about Vikings, including a Viking quest game to play.
www.bbc.co.uk/education/vikings
BBC website especially for children.
www.bl.uk/onlinegallery/sacredtexts/lindisfarne.html
See the original Lindisfarne Gospels online.
www.iomguide.com
Find out about Viking sites around the Isle of Man

Note to parents and teachers
Every effort has been made by the Publishers to ensure that the websites in this book are suitable for children, that they are of the highest educational value, and that they contain no inappropriate or offensive material. However, because of the nature of the Internet, it is impossible to guarantee that the contents of these sites will not be altered. We strongly advise that Internet access is supervised by a responsible adult.

INDEX

Here are the lists of contents for each title in *Tracking Down...*